P9-DOH-220

DATE DUE			

ANCIENT CULTURES AND CIVILIZATIONS

THE CULTURE OF THE

BYZANTINE EMPIRE

Vic Kovacs

PowerKiDS
press™

NEW YORK

Published in 2017 by **The Rosen Publishing Group, Inc.**
29 East 21st Street, New York, NY 10010

Cataloging-in-Publication Data

Names: Kovacs, Vic.
Title: The culture of the Byzantine Empire / Vic Kovacs.
Description: New York : PowerKids Press, 2017. | Series: Ancient cultures and civilizations | Includes index.
Identifiers: ISBN 9781508150060 (pbk.) | ISBN 9781508150015 (library bound) | ISBN 9781508149927 (6 pack)
Subjects: LCSH: Byzantine Empire--Social life and customs--Juvenile literature. | Byzantine Empire--
    Civilization--Juvenile literature.
Classification: LCC DF521.K68 2017| DDC 949.5'02--dc23

Copyright © 2017 by The Rosen Publishing Group

All rights reserved. No part of this book may be reproduced in any form
without permission in writing from the publisher, except by a reviewer.

Developed and produced for Rosen by BlueAppleWorks Inc.

Art Director: Haley Harasymiw
Managing Editor for BlueAppleWorks: Melissa McClellan
Editors: Janice Dyer, Marcia Abramson
Design: T.J. Choleva

Picture credits: p. 7 PavleMarjanovic/Shutterstock; p. 8 Adbar/Creative Commons; p. 8 inset AridOcean/
Shutterstock; p. 9 dinosmichail/Shutterstock; p. 10 inset Mikhail Markovskiy/Shutterstock; p. 10 Mehmet
Cetin/Shutterstock; p. 11 inset left, 11 mountainpix/Shutterstock; p. 11 inset right Jahrhunderts/Public
Domain; p. 12 Alberto Pasini /Public Domain; p. 15 Petar Milošević/Creative Commons; p. 18 Renata
Sedmakova/Shutterstock; p. 19 Viktor M. Vasnetsov/Public Domain; p. 21 Otto Albert Koch/Public Domain;
p. 22 Ulpiano Checa/Public Domain; p. 23 Edwin Lord Weeks/Public Domain; p. 24 Public Domain;
p. 27 Jean-Joseph Benjamin-Constant/Public Domain; p. 28 Raffael/Public Domain; p. 29 Berkomaster/
Shutterstock; Maps: p. 5 T.J. Choleva/Shutterstock: adike

Manufactured in the United States of America
CPSIA Compliance Information: Batch #BS16PK: For Further Information contact Rosen Publishing, New York, New York at 1-800-237-9932

BRISTOW MIDDLE SCHOOL

3 2547 16038426

CONTENTS

CHAPTER 1

THE BYZANTINE EMPIRE

The Byzantine Empire began as the eastern part of the Roman Empire. Although its background was Roman, it outlasted the western Roman Empire and became a unique society greatly influenced by Greek elements.

The center of the empire was its capital city, Constantinople. The city was located on the same site as the ancient Greek settlement known as Byzantium. The city was founded in 330 by the eastern Roman emperor Constantine I. Constantinople would eventually become the biggest and richest city in Europe.

Though today it's known as the Byzantine Empire, that name wasn't used at the time the empire existed. Instead it was known as the Eastern Roman Empire or the Empire of Romans. Most people living there considered themselves Roman, though many spoke Greek instead of Latin, the traditional language of the Romans.

Through the centuries, the Byzantine Empire would become the most powerful empire in Europe. Byzantine territory included Greek islands, parts of **Asia Minor**, as well as parts of the Balkans, and even Africa. After the fall of the western part of the Roman Empire in 476, Byzantine rulers extended the Roman Empire's reign in the east until 1453, when Constantinople fell to Ottoman invaders.

Europe

Balkans

Asia Minor

■ The Byzantine Empire at
its peak around A.D. 550

Africa

At its peak, the Byzantine Empire was
the most powerful economic, cultural,
and **military** force in Europe.

5

CHAPTER 2

CONSTANTINOPLE— THE CITY OF THE WORLD

Constantine I became the head of both the eastern and western parts of the Roman Empire after he won a series of military battles. He needed a new location for the reunited empire's capital. The site he chose had been an ancient Greek city called Byzantium. Constantine chose this location because Rome had been slowly falling into disrepair, and he wanted something new, something all his own. The site of old Byzantium had many things in its favor. It was surrounded by water, so it was fairly easy to protect from invaders. It was located on a land bridge between Greece and Asia, and connected the empire's territories in those regions. The waterway known as the Golden Horn also created an incredible harbor, which, combined with its location, helped to make it a major trading port.

It took six years to build the new city of Constantinople, or the New Rome as the emperor called it. The city was finished and **consecrated** in 330. It is claimed that Constantine designed the city himself.

MARKING THE EMPIRE'S CENTER

Early in the fourth century, a monument called the Milion was built in Constantinople. It marked the starting place for measuring distances to the cities in the Byzantine Empire.

Roman Emperor Constantine I founded the city of Constantinople. This mosaic shows him holding a miniature model of the city he built.

The city was built atop seven hills, just like the old Rome. Also like Rome, it was divided into fourteen regions. The city was filled with awe-inspiring architecture, such as the Augusteum, a square at its center, and the Great Palace of the Empire just south of the square. Beautiful statues of important figures from Roman history and **mythology** were located throughout the city.

As Constantinople became a more important city, the rulers focused on improving its defenses. The emperor Theodosius II built three layers of massive, 60-foot-tall (18 m) walls between 413 and 414. These walls protected the city from every attack until the invention of gunpowder. By 476, when Rome finally fell and the last western Roman emperor was **deposed** by **barbarians**, Constantinople had become the biggest and most important city of the empire.

Constantinople was built on the Bosphorus strait. This waterway separates Europe from Asia.

A ring of 14 miles (22.5 km) of walls protected the city of Constantinople. The walls were made of stones, limestone, and brick, held together with mortar. The walls included more than 400 towers and bastions.

BYZANTINE ARCHITECTURE

During this period, the influence of Rome decreased. Instead, the Byzantine Empire became the center of architectural know-how and sophistication. Like many aspects of their culture, Byzantine architecture used elements from both Greek and Roman styles and combined them to create something completely new.

Byzantine architects were famous for constructing magnificent religious buildings and churches. Byzantine architecture was so popular that buildings based on Byzantine originals still exist all over Europe today. The famous St. Mark's Basilica in Venice is just one example of this. City walls and defensive structures of many cities in Europe were also inspired by the Byzantine building methods and styles.

The most impressive of Byzantine churches was the Hagia Sophia. Commissioned by the emperor Justinian I, it took over five years to build, from 532 to 537. Justinian spared no expense. A workforce of 10,000 men was hired to build the church. Materials such as gold, marble, and jewels were imported from different countries and continents including Egypt, Greece, and Syria. Once completed, it was the largest cathedral in the world for just under a thousand years.

Originally built as a Greek Orthodox church, it served as a Roman Catholic church between 1204 and 1261, when it again became the home of the Patriarch of Constantinople, the head of the Greek Orthodox Church. It traded hands between religions again in 1453, when it became a mosque under the orders of the Muslim conqueror Sultan Mehmed II. Hagia Sophia was turned into a museum in 1935. Today it attracts over three million visitors each year.

Hagia Sophia is best known for its huge dome, but the interior was also praised for its remarkable beauty.

Ancient paintings and mosaics often showed scenes from peasant life.

PEOPLE OF CONSTANTINOPLE

Much of Byzantine society was involved in agriculture. Members of the peasant class generally made their livings as shepherds and farmers. They lived outside of cities in smaller villages, where they grew crops and raised livestock. Important crops included grain and beans, as well as the Mediterranean staples of olives and grapes for wine. Byzantine peasants were also famous for their beekeeping and honey production, a skill that survived in the countryside from the times of ancient Greece. The peasants provided the empire with a steady supply of food, which allowed the rest of Byzantine society to grow and thrive.

Merchants came from all over to buy and sell their products in the Constantinople markets.

Constantinople was a major trading point, so merchants also became more and more important and powerful. Their economic influence spread all over the world. Markets as far away as Cairo and Alexandria in Egypt, and elsewhere, often had to adjust the prices of products to match the trading that took place in Constantinople. Successful merchants were even allowed to join the senate, which gave them an important role in guiding the policy of the empire.

Another important class in Byzantine society was the **clergy**. Priests weren't separated from the rest of society as much as their counterparts in the Roman Catholic Church were. Another important difference was that lower priests were allowed to have wives, as long as they had been married before they entered the priesthood. More powerful officials, like bishops, were expected to be single.

CENTER OF THE WORLD'S TRADE

Constantinople was a major economic center. Because of its location and importance as the empire's capital, people came from all over to buy and sell just about everything. Merchants from China and India brought spices, while Russian merchants traded leather, wax, and caviar. Gold and silk products were likely the most popular items in the city's many marketplaces. The local government regulated exactly how many foreign traders were allowed into the city at any one time. Despite the fact that Constantinople was a Christian city, people from all races and faiths were welcome to do business. Arabs, Jews, Russians, and Italians all took part in trade. While in the city, they were housed in specific areas. The Golden Rule for trade in Constantinople was simple: nothing could be bought or sold if there was a chance it might go toward helping an enemy of the empire.

EDUCATION

Education was widely available in the Byzantine Empire. As a result, much of the Byzantine population was able to read and write. Most boys and girls attended elementary schools, which were available even in the countryside. However, secondary schools only existed in bigger cities. The schools were generally better than those in the west, at least until the twelfth century when educational centers in western Europe began to improve. Higher learning was only available in the metropolis of Constantinople. There, students were instructed in law, philosophy, and medicine. Future members of the empire's bureaucracy were taught necessary skills in the state school system.

CHAPTER 3

SEAT OF CHRISTIAN EMPERORS

The Byzantine Empire was ruled by the emperor, who was believed to have received his powers from God. The emperor was the leader of many administrators and **bureaucrats** who did the day-to-day work that made the empire run smoothly.

Constantine I wanted to make Christianity the only religion of the empire, but he did not fully succeed. However, he did help to increase its popularity. A later emperor, Julian the Apostate, was known as the last **pagan** emperor. He tried to outlaw Christianity and remove all traces of the Christian church, but he failed. Christianity was finally made the official state religion by Emperor Theodosius the Great in 391, when paganism was completely outlawed.

Emperor Justinian, who ruled from 527 to 565, was one of the most important Byzantine rulers. He is best remembered for creating a series of legal reforms known as the Justinian Code. Justinian built new roads, bridges, and aqueducts that greatly improved the lives of Byzantine citizens. He was also a great patron of Byzantine arts, including theater and music. One of his most trusted advisers was his wife, Theodora. Many believed that she was responsible for the laws that supported the rights of women. During his reign, Emperor Justinian added Spain, Italy, and North Africa to the empire's territory.

Emperor Justinian was also known as Justinian the Great. His goals were to return the empire to greatness and reconquer the western provinces of the Roman Empire.

CHRISTIANITY OF BYZANTINE EMPIRE

Christianity was an essential part of the Byzantine Empire. Byzantine emperors were also known as the Caesaropapist, which meant that they were rulers of both the state and the church. Just underneath the emperor was the bishop of Constantinople, who was later called the patriarch.

As Constantinople grew, it became a center of Christianity, competing in importance with Rome. When **Islam** became the dominant religion in the Middle East, Rome and Constantinople became the leaders of Christian thought. Both cities had certain ideas about the development of the church. At the end, both cities established their individual branches of Christianity.

The increasing number of differences between the two Christian centers soon became problematic. Some of these differences, like the fact that Rome spoke Latin and Constantinople spoke Greek, were fairly **superficial**. There were, however, differences in religious belief that were more difficult to overcome. The largest of these was the Iconoclast Movement. Rome, which had used **icons** in their worship for generations, believed they should continue to do so. They did not appreciate Byzantines telling them that they were wrong.

ICONOCLAST MOVEMENT

Byzantine emperors felt that icons were not worthy of worship. The movement supporting this idea was called Iconoclasm, meaning "the smashing of icons." This major disagreement between the eastern and western churches was resolved in 843, when it was agreed that religious icons are an important part of worship.

GREEK CUSTOMS

The Byzantine Empire grew out of Roman roots. Its laws and the structure of its government were originally Roman. However, although the official language was Latin, many of the people who lived there spoke Greek. Children learned all about Greek culture. As the years went on, Rome's influence decreased. Some historians point to the differences between the eastern and western churches as the major cause of this. By 610, when Heraclius became emperor, Rome had even less influence on the Byzantine Empire. The new emperor officially made Greek the state language, and within forty years the empire was much more Greek than Roman. This even included the way their soldiers fought. The strategies that the soldiers used were more similar to those used by the ancient Greek cities of Sparta and Athens than to those of the Roman Legions.

The most serious conflict grew out of Rome's desire to be the only leader of all of Christianity. The Byzantine patriarchs disagreed with this concept. The fight grew so intense that both the pope and the patriarch banished each other from the church in what came to be known as the Great Schism of 1054. Their refusal to recognize the other's authority led to the formation of the Roman Catholic Church in the west and the Greek Orthodox Church in the east. Even today, the two churches have different forms of worship. The formation of the Greek Orthodox Church is probably one of the biggest contributions of the Byzantine Empire to the world.

ORTHODOX MISSIONARIES

Byzantine society had a deep effect on people in nearby territories, especially on Slavic people. Serbs and Croats arrived in the region in the sixth century, followed by Bulgars who settled in the Danube River valley. In the early stages, the relationship between Byzantians and their Slavic neighbors was uneasy. However, Byzantine **diplomacy** eventually smoothed the tensions between the two groups.

Much of this was done through **missionary** work. Orthodox missionaries from the Byzantine Empire traveled into Slavic lands to introduce their religion and to convert the pagan Slavs to their faith. Two missionaries, today known as St. Cyril and St. Methodius, even created an entire alphabet for the Slavs. The alphabet, which used Greek letters, is known as the Cyrillic alphabet, and is still used today.

Cyril and Methodius were brothers born into a noble Greek family. They became missionaries who brought Christianity to Slavic peoples.

Vladimir the Great was the grand prince of Kiev. In 988, he started the process to bring Orthodox Christianity to the lands that became Russia.

This allowed the missionaries to translate Greek religious texts into Slavic versions that could be easily be understood by Slavs. St. Cyril and St. Methodius also organized schools that taught children Christianity, as well as reading and writing.

The missionaries traveled widely, doing their most important work in Moravia and in the Bulgarian Empire. Cyrillic writing and Orthodox Christianity spread through all Slavic lands, reaching all the way to vast Russian lands. Russian leaders would later go on to found the Russian Orthodox Church, which is based on Byzantine foundations.

STS. CYRIL AND METHODIUS LEGACY

Languages that use the Cyrillic alphabet today include Russian, Bulgarian, Serbian, and Ukrainian.

CHAPTER 4

STRUGGLES FOR SUPREMACY

The Byzantine Empire faced the ongoing challenge of keeping friendly relationships with all their neighbors. This became even more important after Rome fell. Their neighbors included various Germanic peoples, Huns, Slavs, Arabs, Persians, and others. The empire's main ways for dealing with its neighbors were the Byzantine army, **navy,** and diplomacy.

For centuries, the Byzantine army was one of the best in both Europe and Asia. Although based on Rome's army, it changed over the years. By about the seventh century, it depended on **cavalry**. This made the Byzantine army much more similar to the militaries of ancient Greeks than to Roman Legions. One key similarity to the Roman army that remained was the use of foreign **mercenaries**.

As strong as the Byzantine army was, though, the main reason for the empire's long survival was the use of clever diplomatic tricks. Constantinople had many foreign embassies, and diplomats there were encouraged to stay for years at a time. These diplomats served multiple uses. If their home territory was being troublesome, they could be threatened or held hostage. If the empire wanted something from their homelands, they could be used to influence its rulers. The empire also used **propaganda**, shocking foreigners with displays of wealth and gold, and convincing them of the importance of the empire.

The Western Roman Empire fell in 476. After this, the Byzantine Empire was continuously threatened by a flood of hostile neighbors who took turns trying to destroy the empire.

BYZANTINE EMPIRE AND BARBARIAN HORDES

Invasion from **hordes** of barbarians was a major threat for all Roman territory from 376 to about 800. Early hordes were made up of Germanic tribes, including Goths, Saxons, and Vandals, and the Romans were later forced west by Huns, Bulgars, Slavs, and others. This constant attack would eventually lead to the fall of the Western Roman Empire.

Leaders in the east dealt with the barbarian threat in many different ways. When necessary, the army and the navy were called to defeat and crush the barbarian invaders. They also used diplomatic strategies, including providing the barbarians with large sums of money and gold in exchange for a short-lived peace agreement. Byzantians were also experts in turning their various enemies against each other, leaving them too busy to trouble the empire.

Barbarian warriors of different tribes spent almost as much time fighting each other as they did fighting Rome and Byzantium.

Agents of the Office of Barbarian Affairs often had other jobs, such as merchants, which gave them a reason to visit foreign lands.

FOREIGN INTELLIGENCE AGENCY

Some historians believe that the Byzantine Empire was home to the first foreign intelligence agency. The Office of Barbarian Affairs, also known as the Bureau of Barbarians, existed on its surface to protect foreign **dignitaries**. It also provided translation services. The bureau asked its agents to closely watch visiting **envoys'** servants to make sure they were not gathering information about the empire from locals. This is certainly an early example of counter-intelligence. Byzantine envoys sent abroad also gathered information about the empire's neighbors that might prove useful, including facts about their customs, politics, and leaders. These fact-finding missions could be quite long, sometimes even lasting years. In those cases, envoys would send back written reports.

BYZANTINE EMPIRE AND ISLAM

In the 630s, Byzantine lost much of its southern territory to Muslim Arabs. These provinces included Syria and Egypt. This led to a long period of fighting between the empire and Muslims, with repeated raids into Byzantine lands. In fact, the invading Muslims nearly captured Constantinople twice! Fighting continued until the Arabs were defeated during the Second Arab Siege of Constantinople in 718. These battles would come to be known as the Arab-Byzantine Wars.

The First Arab Siege of Constantinople took place between 674 and 678. During those four years, the Arab navy set up bases for their fleets of ships on the coast across from Constantinople. The Arabs tried to cut off Constantinople by land and sea to stop it from accessing its supply bases.

Devices spewing Greek fire as shown on this ancient Byzantine manuscript were probably similar to modern military flamethrowers.

GREEK FIRE

Greek fire was a secret weapon created and used by the Byzantine navy. It was an incredibly destructive material that burst into flames as soon as it touched water. During battle, it would be blasted onto enemy ships from tubes mounted on Byzantine boats. Once it caught fire, it was nearly impossible to put out, and could even burn on top of water. The recipe was kept secret, and remains unknown today. What is known is that it helped the empire to win many battles. Without Greek fire, the two Arab Sieges of Constantinople may have ended with the city's fall.

Each spring during the siege, the Arab armies attacked directly and tried to destroy the walls surrounding Constantinople. After four years under siege, the empire, under the leadership of Emperor Constantine IV, finally smashed the Arab naval forces with a new weapon called Greek fire. This, along with victory against the Muslim army in Asia Minor, ended the siege and began a brief era of peace.

By 717, however, the Arabs were at it again. The Second Arab Siege of Constantinople ended in 718, thanks again to Greek fire. Famine, illness, and a harsh winter helped the Byzantines defeat the Muslim forces. Arab armies were also distracted by constant attacks by Bulgars. This second failure to take the Byzantine capital had lasting effects. Muslim forces gave up on conquering the empire, though lesser attacks still happened regularly. Today, the battle is considered hugely important, because it stopped Muslim movement into southeastern Europe for hundreds of years.

CHAPTER 5

DECLINE, FALL, AND LEGACY

Though the Byzantine Empire was mighty, it was not **invincible**. During the Fourth Crusade in the thirteenth century, Constantinople was sacked and taken over by the army of crusaders. The crusaders' original aim was to seize Egypt, then the most powerful area in the Muslim world. However, they were tricked into attacking Constantinople. The crusaders replaced the Byzantine emperor and the patriarch with their own, and started what they called the Latin Empire. This new empire only lasted from 1204 to 1261, when the city was taken back by the Byzantine leaders. Though the Byzantine Empire was restored, it lost most of its former glory and power.

The Byzantine Empire fell for good on Tuesday, May 29, 1453. On that day, Constantinople was taken by Sultan Mehmed II, after a fifty-day siege. The once great city could only raise 10,000 men to defend it. The invading Muslim Turks had at least ten times that number. They smashed the city's famous walls to bits with cannon fire, and their much larger army quickly overran the city. The city's location was perfect for Mehmed II to mount extensive military actions against Europe. To signal the beginning of a new era, the sultan changed the name of the city to Istanbul.

When Mehmed II entered Constantinople, he immediately rode his horse to the Hagia Sophia to prevent soldiers from destroying it.

The conquered city was fully claimed for Islam, but citizens were allowed to keep practicing Christianity. They were forbidden to own weapons, though, and were forced to dress in clothes that immediately identified them as non-Muslims. With the end of Constantinople came the end of the last bit of the Roman Empire, after more than a thousand years and a great many accomplishments.

LEGACY OF THE BYZANTINE EMPIRE

Much of Byzantine society was based on the works of the great minds of ancient Greece. They preserved many of these works and passed them on, which is a big part of why we still have access to them today. They also helped to translate many of these works into more modern languages. After the fall of the empire, many Byzantine scholars moved to Italy, where they continued to help shape the **Renaissance** culture.

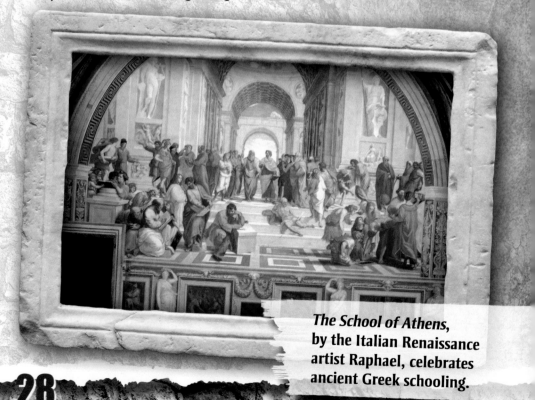

The School of Athens, by the Italian Renaissance artist Raphael, celebrates ancient Greek schooling.

The architecture of Istanbul reflects its Byzantine and Ottoman history. Its buildings also remind us of the peoples and empires that ruled the city.

They also helped to spread Arabic science to Italy. Innovations in fields such as art and technology are still important to us thanks to these Byzantines.

The Orthodox Church was one of the empire's largest contributions to the world, and is one of the longest lasting. Even today, the legacy of the empire can be seen in many countries where Orthodox Christianity is still the main religion, such as Greece, Russia, Serbia, and many more. The same legacy continues in countries where people use the Cyrillic alphabet as the official alphabet for their national languages. In this way, the empire that fell more than five hundred years ago still lives on.

GLOSSARY

Asia Minor: a peninsula that extends from Asia close to Europe, where modern-day Turkey is located

barbarians: according to the Byzantine people, any foreigners of non-Roman descent

bastion: part of a fortification

bureaucrat: an administrator in any kind of organization

cavalry: a branch of the military trained to fight on horseback

clergy: a class of religious priests

consecrate: to give a type of blessing that elevates something to sacred status

depose: to remove from office

dignitary: an important official

diplomacy: negotiating using peaceful means

envoy: a government representative

horde: a large group

icon: a sacred image or picture

invincible: unable to be defeated

Islam: a religion that believes the teachings of the prophet Muhammad. Its followers are called Muslims.

mercenary: a soldier hired for service in a foreign army

military: an organized group of soldiers who protect and fight for the interests of a city, state, or country

missionary: a person who tries to convert people to a religion

mythology: the collection of stories that explain a people's history, heroes, and origin

navy: a branch of the military concerned with battles on bodies of water such as the ocean

pagan: a person without religion

propaganda: organized information to help the cause of the government

Renaissance: the transition from medieval to modern times that took place from the fourteenth through sixteenth century

superficial: minor or not important

FOR MORE INFORMATION

Books

Blattner, Don. *World Civilizations and Cultures.*
Greensboro, NC : Mark Twain Media, 2012.

Rodgers, Kelly. *The Byzantine Empire: A Society That Shaped the World.*
Huntington Beach, CA: Teacher Created Materials, 2012.

VanVoorst, Jennifer Fretland. *The Byzantine Empire:*
(*Exploring the Ancient World.*)
Mankato, MN: Compass Point Books, 2012.

Websites

Due to the changing nature of Internet links, PowerKids Press has developed an online list of websites related to the subject of this book. This site is updated regularly. Please use this link to access the list:

www.powerkidslinks.com/acc/byzan

INDEX